THE CAVAPOO WAY:

A GUIDE TO

SUCCESSFUL DOG

OWNERSHIP

MASTER THE ART OF RAISING,
TRAINING, AND CARING FOR
YOUR CAVAPOO

GUS TALES

CONTENTS

FOREWORD

Hello, fellow dog lovers!

It is a pleasure to welcome you to "The Cavapoo Way: A Guide to Successful Dog Ownership." My name is Gus Tales. I can personally attest to the happiness and companionship these amazing dogs bring to our lives as the proud owner of Isabel, a 5-year-old ruby Cavapoo. I have acquired a great deal of knowledge about the distinct Cavapoo culture over the years, and I am eager to impart that knowledge to you in this extensive guide. Through this book, I hope to provide you with the knowledge and skills necessary to successfully navigate the rewarding journey of Cavapoo parenthood.

I've worked with a group of professionals, including veterinarians, cynologists, and experts in canine behavior, to bring you the most accurate and beneficial information possible. These experts have contributed their in-depth knowledge and experience to make sure that this manual accurately reflects a comprehensive and all-encompassing approach to Cavapoo ownership.

The chapters that follow contain a wealth of knowledge on all facets of Cavapoo care, from their history and distinguishing traits to the crucial procedures and routines required to ensure a happy coexistence. This book will lead you through the selection of the ideal puppy or adoption of a rescue Cavapoo, as well as the preparation of your home, the establishment of routines, and the development of a strong, loving relationship with your new canine companion. We'll also go into great detail about senior Cavapoo care, including its special challenges and rewards, as well as proper nutrition, health care, grooming, training, exercise, and mental stimulation.

Finally, we will look at the larger Cavapoo community, including clubs, events, and local and online resources that can make owning a Cavapoo more enjoyable. Throughout your journey with your cherished

Cavapoo, this group of like-minded individuals will be a great source of encouragement, counsel, and camaraderie.

Always keep in mind the value of love, patience, and consistency as you set out on this thrilling adventure with your Cavapoo. These traits will not only strengthen your relationship with your dog but also open the door to a lifetime of joy and understanding.

Let's start this incredible adventure together, and I hope you and your Cavapoo have a lifetime of happiness, love, and companionship. Welcome to "The Cavapoo Way."

Sincerely,

Gus Tales & Isabel the Cavapoo

CHAPTER 1:

INTRODUCTION TO CAVAPOOS

CHAPTER 1:
INTRODUCTION TO CAVAPOOS

We are grateful that you decided to pick up a copy of "The Cavapoo Way: A Guide to Successful Dog Ownership" and that you took the time to learn more about Cavapoos. In this extensive guide, we will discuss all of the most important aspects of bringing up, training, and caring for your cherished Cavapoo. In this introductory chapter, we will investigate the background of the Cavapoo breed, investigate its history, determine the characteristics that set it apart from other dog breeds, and talk about the many benefits and drawbacks of owning a Cavapoo.

THE DEVELOPMENT OF THE BREED & ITS WIDESPREAD POPULARITY

In the latter half of the 20th century, the designer hybrid breed known as the Cavapoo, also spelled cavapoo, Cavadoodle, and Cavoodle, made its debut for the first time. The breeding of a Cavalier King Charles Spaniel and a Poodle produced this dog breed, which is affectionate, small, sociable, perceptive, and boasts a hypoallergenic coat. Other desirable characteristics of this breed include its small size. Although the Cavapoo was first developed in Australia, its popularity quickly spread to other parts of the world, specifically the United States and Europe.

The cute and cuddly appearance of the Cavapoo has undeniably been a major contributor to the breed's meteoric rise in popularity. These adorable dogs are nearly impossible to say no to due to their expressive eyes, floppy ears, and wavy to curly fur. They are sure to win your heart. In addition, because of their kind and loving demeanor, they make wonderful companions not only for retirees but also for single people and families. Cavapoos are also well-known for their gentle demeanor toward both children and other animals, which further contributes to the Cavapoo's status as an ideal canine companion for families.

UNDERSTANDING CAVAPOO GENERATIONS

When you first start your search for a Cavapoo puppy, you'll likely come across terms like "F1", "F1b", "F2", and so on. These are designations that describe the specific generation of a Cavapoo, and they can have an impact on your pup's characteristics, including size, coat type, and overall health. Understanding what these designations mean will help you make a more informed decision when choosing your new companion.

First Generation Cavapoos (F1)

First-generation Cavapoos, often written as "F1", are the result of breeding a purebred Cavalier King Charles Spaniel with a purebred Poodle. The aim is to produce puppies that exhibit the desirable traits of both parent breeds. F1 Cavapoos tend to have a more predictable size and appearance than later generations. They also benefit from a genetic principle known as hybrid vigor, which suggests that mixed-breed dogs are generally healthier and live longer than their purebred counterparts due to greater genetic diversity.

Second Generation Cavapoos (F1b and F2)

F1b Cavapoos are produced when an F1 Cavapoo is bred back with a purebred Poodle. This increases the Poodle genetics to 75%, which often results in a curlier coat, making this generation a good choice for those with allergies.

F2 Cavapoos, on the other hand, are the result of breeding two F1 Cavapoos together. While F2 puppies can still make excellent pets, their traits can be less predictable. For example, their coat may vary from straight to wavy to curly within the same litter.

Third Generation and Beyond (F2b, F3, and so on)

As we go further down the generations, the designations can get more complex. For instance, an F2b Cavapoo is the offspring of an F1 Cavapoo and an F1b Cavapoo. Similarly, F3 Cavapoos are the result of breeding two F2 Cavapoos together.

It's important to note that as you go further down the generations, the predictability of size, appearance, and coat type can decrease. However, if bred responsibly, these Cavapoos can still be healthy, wonderful pets.

Choosing the Right Generation

Ultimately, the best generation for you will depend on your personal preferences and lifestyle. If you have severe allergies, you might prefer an F1b Cavapoo due to their typically curlier, more hypoallergenic coat. If you're more interested in the Cavalier King Charles Spaniel's appearance, an F1 Cavapoo might be a better fit.

Keep in mind that every dog is unique, and their behavior and temperament will be influenced not only by their genetic makeup but also by their upbringing, socialization, and training. So, while understanding Cavapoo generations is helpful, it's only one piece of the puzzle when selecting your new best friend.

PARENT BREEDS: A QUICK HISTORY

Understanding the parent breeds of the Cavapoo – the Cavalier King Charles Spaniel and the Toy or Miniature Poodle – provides a unique insight into their characteristics and temperament.

The Cavalier King Charles Spaniel

Originating from the United Kingdom, the Cavalier King Charles Spaniel boasts a rich history. Named after King Charles II of England, who was very fond of the breed, these dogs were often seen in the arms of royal ladies in the 17th century. Known for their affectionate nature and charming personalities, Cavalier King Charles Spaniels are incredibly friendly and sociable.

The Toy/Miniature Poodle

The Poodle, on the other hand, has roots in Germany but gained its fame in France. Poodles come in three sizes: Standard, Miniature, and Toy. The Miniature and Toy Poodles are the ones commonly crossbred with Cavalier King Charles Spaniels to create Cavapoos. Poodles are known for their high intelligence, agility, and hypoallergenic coats, making them popular in crossbreeding programs.

CHARACTERISTICS THAT SET CAVAPOOS APART

Cavapoos are classified as small dogs because they typically have a shoulder height ranging from 9 to 14 inches (22 to 35 cm) and a weight ranging from 12 to 25 pounds (5 to 12 kg). Cavapoos can stand between 9 and 14 inches (22 to 35 cm) tall. Their coats can be found in a number of different colors, including chocolate, black, apricot, ruby and cream. The fur on a Cavapoo can have a variety of different textures, ranging from curly to wavy, and the breed may shed very little. However, they are typically regarded as hypoallergenic and have a low shedding rate, which makes them an excellent choice for people who suffer from allergies.

Cavalier King Charles Spaniels and Poodles are the two breeds that give birth to Cavapoos. These dogs owe their cleverness, eagerness to please, and ease of training to the fact that their ancestors were Poodles. The affectionate, calm, and outgoing nature, combined with the intelligence of the Cavalier King Charles Spaniel, make these dogs wonderful companions. Cavapoos are renowned for their adaptability, and as a result, they are able to do well in a diverse range of living environments, from smaller apartments to houses with large yards.

HYBRID VIGOR IN CAVAPOOS

Hybrid vigor, also known as heterosis, is a concept in genetics where mixed-breed animals tend to exhibit superior qualities in certain aspects compared to their purebred counterparts. This phenomenon is often seen in Cavapoos and is a crucial factor in their popularity and success as companion animals.

What is Hybrid Vigor?

Hybrid vigor refers to the enhancement of certain biological traits due to mixing diverse genetic backgrounds. When two unrelated breeds are crossed, like the Cavalier King Charles Spaniel and the Poodle, their offspring inherit a combination of genes that can result in better health, greater vitality, and, in some cases, a longer lifespan.

This genetic diversity helps to minimize the risk of inheriting genetic disorders common in purebred dogs, which often suffer from a lack of genetic variation due to generations of inbreeding to maintain breed standards.

Hybrid Vigor in Cavapoos

Cavapoos, as first-generation hybrids (F1), often exhibit strong hybrid vigor. They generally inherit the best traits from both parent breeds and are less likely to inherit breed-specific genetic disorders. For instance, Cavaliers are known for their heart issues, while Poodles are prone to certain eye conditions. A Cavapoo, due to its mixed heritage, is less likely to inherit these specific ailments.

It's important to note that hybrid vigor does not guarantee a perfectly healthy dog. However, it does generally increase the odds of good health compared to purebred dogs.

Limitations of Hybrid Vigor

As we move to later generations of Cavapoos (F1b, F2, etc.), the effects of hybrid vigor can diminish. This is because the genetic diversity decreases when an F1 Cavapoo is bred with another Cavapoo or a purebred Poodle or Cavalier King Charles Spaniel.

Furthermore, while hybrid vigor can reduce the risk of breed-specific diseases, it does not eliminate the possibility of other genetic disorders. This is why it's critical to choose a reputable breeder who health tests their breeding dogs.

The Role of Good Breeding Practices

While hybrid vigor is a compelling factor in the Cavapoo's health, it is not a substitute for responsible breeding practices. A good breeder will prioritize health testing for all breeding dogs to ensure they are not passing on known genetic diseases. They will also prioritize proper socialization, nutrition, and care to promote the overall health and wellbeing of their puppies.

In conclusion, the Cavapoo's hybrid vigor can contribute to its robust health and vitality, making it a desirable breed choice for many dog lovers. However, always remember that good health is not guaranteed solely by a dog's genetic makeup - proper care, nutrition, and regular veterinary check-ups are just as essential in raising a healthy, happy Cavapoo.

***

THE PROS AND CONS OF OWNING A CAVAPOO

Pros:

1. **Temperament:** Cavapoos have a well-deserved reputation for being loving and affectionate, which makes them fantastic pets and cuddle buddies. Their reputation stems from the fact that they are loving and affectionate. They develop deep connections with the human members of their family and have a strong drive to fulfill their masters' wishes.

2. **Allergies:** Cavapoos are an excellent option for people who suffer from allergies because they don't shed very much and produce a significantly lower amount of dander than other breeds of dogs.

3. **Intelligence:** The impressive intelligence of Poodles is passed down to Cavapoos, which gives them a distinct advantage in the canine world. Because of this, they are capable of picking up new information quickly and are not too difficult to instruct.

4. **Adaptability:** Cavapoos are able to adjust well to a wide variety of environments and living conditions, which makes them an excellent choice for both city and country life.

5. **Compatibility** with children and other animals: Because of their outgoing and friendly nature, Cavapoos make fantastic playmates for children as well as other kinds of animals. However, in order to keep younger children safe, it is essential to keep an eye on their interactions with older children.

Cons:

1. **Grooming:** Cavapoos require regular grooming in order to keep their coats in good health and free of tangles. This includes grooming tasks such as brushing, bathing, and trimming as

required. In addition, it is essential for their overall health to have their ears cleaned on a regular basis, their nails trimmed, and their teeth brushed.

2. **Health issues:** Cavapoos, being a hybrid breed, may be more prone to certain health issues, such as hip dysplasia, patellar luxation, and heart problems, when compared to their purebred parent breeds. These health issues include hip dysplasia, patellar luxation, and heart problems.

3. **Separation anxiety:** Cavapoos are prone to developing separation anxiety when they are left alone for extended periods of time, and this anxiety can show itself in the form of undesirable behaviors. It may be possible to alleviate these issues by engaging in regular physical activity and mental stimulation.

4. **Requirements for physical activity:** Because Cavapoos are energetic dogs, they require regular physical activity in order to remain happy and healthy. This entails taking them on daily walks and making sure they get plenty of time to play so that they remain mentally and physically stimulated.

You will be able to determine if a Cavapoo would be a good fit for your family if you educate yourself on the breed's essential characteristics as well as its basic requirements. In the following chapters, we will delve deeper into the specifics of owning a Cavapoo, as well as provide valuable resources to assist you on your journey to becoming a successful and responsible dog owner.

CHAPTER 2:
CHOOSING YOUR CAVAPOO

Now that you are more knowledgeable about the Cavapoo breed, you should concentrate on picking the ideal Cavapoo for you and your family. Finding a reputable breeder, choosing the best puppy for your family, and looking into adoption and rescue options are just a few of the crucial topics covered in this chapter.

HOW TO LOCATE A TRUSTWORTHY BREEDER

Finding a reputable breeder who puts their dogs' health and welfare first is the first step in finding your Cavapoo. The health and temperament of your future Cavapoo will be greatly impacted by the breeder you choose, so it is imperative that you carefully consider your options and take your time. The following advice will help you locate the ideal breeder:

- **Examine prospective breeders:** Get started by learning about local Cavapoo breeders or those who can ship you a puppy. An excellent place to start is with a straightforward internet search. You can also visit breed-specific clubs in your area, go to dog shows, or ask veterinarians, groomers, and other dog owners for recommendations.

- **Seek out warning signs:** Be wary of breeders who have several litters available at once, are unable to give specific information about the parent dogs, or don't place a high priority on health testing. These are red flags that the breeder might not care about the welfare of their dogs.

- **Health evaluations:** For the purpose of identifying potential genetic problems and preventing their transmission, a reputable breeder will conduct health tests on the breeding dogs and puppies. Make sure the breeder you choose tests their dogs for conditions like hip dysplasia, patellar luxation, and heart problems that are frequently found in Cavapoos.

— **Check out the breeder:** It's imperative to go to the breeder's location and, if possible, meet the parent dogs. This gives you the chance to look around the living quarters, evaluate the temperament of the parent dogs, and decide whether the breeder is sincere about caring for their dogs' welfare.

— **Ask questions:** Asking the breeder about their breeding program, their experience with Cavapoos, and their views on how to care for and train dogs is completely acceptable. A trustworthy breeder will be delighted to respond to your inquiries and offer any necessary details.

— **Breeding expertise:** A good breeder will have knowledge of the breed and be eager to inform prospective buyers about the special characteristics of Cavapoos, such as their requirements for grooming, exercise, and training.

— **Support and advice:** A reputable breeder will care about the long-term welfare of their puppies and should be prepared to offer new owners ongoing support and direction. They must also be prepared to take the dog back if you are unable to care for it for any reason.

HOW TO CHOOSE
THE BEST PUPPY FOR YOUR FAMILY

When you have located a trustworthy breeder, it is time to select the ideal Cavapoo puppy for your household. When choosing a puppy, a number of factors should be taken into account, such as temperament, energy level, and appearance.

- **Look at the litter:** Spend some time watching the pups interacting with their surroundings and one another. A puppy with a balanced personality—one that is neither overly timid nor overly assertive—is what you should seek out. A puppy with good socialization should be curious, engaging, and self-assured around people.

- **Test the temperament:** Talk to the breeder about conducting temperament assessments on the puppies. This can assist you in choosing the puppy that most closely fits your preferences and way of life. Observing the pups' responses to various stimuli, such as loud noises, unfamiliar objects, and being held and touched, is one of the tests.

- **Energy level:** When choosing a puppy, take into account your lifestyle and level of activity. A Cavapoo with more energy may be what you want if you enjoy hiking and long walks and are very active. On the other hand, a calmer puppy might be more suitable if you favor a more relaxed way of life and shorter walks.

- **Coat color and type:** Although choosing a puppy shouldn't be based primarily on appearance, you might have preferences for the coat type and color. Discuss the breeder's breeding program's potential colors and coat types as well as the likelihood that the coats of the puppies will change as they mature.

- **Gender:** Consider whether a male or female Cavapoo would suit you better. There may be slight variations in size and behavior between the sexes, though there are no appreciable differences in temperament.

— **Family dynamics:** Choosing a puppy that has been socialized with children and other animals is crucial if you have young children or other pets. When you visit, ask the breeder about the puppies' socialization experiences and watch how they behave around your family.

— **Developmental milestones:** It's important to pick a puppy that has accomplished the proper milestones for their age. Consult the breeder about the development, socialization, and health of the puppies, and make sure they have received all necessary shots and veterinary care.

OPTIONS FOR ADOPTION AND RESCUE

Adopting a Cavapoo is a wonderful alternative to buying one from a reputable breeder, though both methods are common. A Cavapoo can find a loving forever home through adoption as an alternative to purchasing from a breeder.

— **Local animal shelters:** Start by getting in touch with your neighborhood's animal shelters and rescue groups. While finding a Cavapoo in a shelter might not be as common, it is still possible, and you might also find other mixed breeds that would make wonderful additions to your family.

— **Breed-specific rescues:** Look for Cavapoo, Poodle, and Cavalier King Charles Spaniel rescue organizations because they occasionally have Cavapoos up for adoption. These groups can assist you in finding a dog that fits your preferences and lifestyle because they have a wealth of knowledge about the breed.

— **Internet sources:** You can look for available dogs on websites like Petfinder and Adopt-a-Pet by selecting the breed, size, and location criteria. These websites can assist you in locating Cavapoos and other comparable breeds that are up for adoption nearby.

— **Be patient and persistent:** Since Cavapoos are a popular breed and available dogs may be quickly adopted, it may take patience and perseverance to find a Cavapoo through adoption. Be ready to wait, keep checking in with shelters and rescue groups, and be willing to think about other breeds or mixed breeds that might fit your lifestyle.

Finally, choosing the best Cavapoo for your family requires careful thought and research. Finding the ideal match for your lifestyle and preferences before making your decision to buy a puppy from a reputable breeder or adopt a dog in need will ensure a successful and satisfying experience as a dog owner. We will offer advice on setting up routines, developing a bond with your new Cavapoo, and caring for them in the upcoming chapters.

CHAPTER 3:
CAVAPOO-PROOFING
YOUR HOME

It's incredibly exciting to bring home a new Cavapoo puppy or a rescue animal. However, it's crucial to take the required actions to establish a secure and comfortable environment in order to ensure a seamless transition for both you and your new dog. This chapter will cover all aspects of Cavapoo-proofing your home, from spotting potential dangers to creating the ideal living environment.

MAKING A COMFORTABLE AND SAFE ENVIRONMENT

1. Recognizing Potential Risks

Identifying and reducing potential hazards is necessary to create a safe environment for your Cavapoo. Get close to your dog and start by scanning the area of your home for potential hazards. The following are some typical household dangers to be aware of:

a. *Electrical Cords and Outlets:* Puppies have a tendency to chew things, which can be dangerous when it comes to electrical cords. To keep cords out of the way or unattractive for chewing, invest in cord protectors or organizers. To avoid accidental shocks, cover unused electrical outlets with outlet covers.

b. *Human Food and Medicine:* Dogs may be poisoned by a variety of human foods and medicines. Ensure that all food and medications are kept out of your Cavapoo's reach and securely stored. Chocolate, grapes, onions, and alcohol are a few common foods to avoid.

c. *Cleaning products:* These products can seriously endanger your pet because they frequently contain harmful chemicals. All cleaning supplies should be locked away in cabinets or kept up high and out of the way.

d. *Small Objects:* Commonplace objects like coins, buttons, and jewelry can cause choking. Keep these things out of your Cavapoo's reach by being careful.

e. *Trash Cans:* To prevent your Cavapoo from digging through and consuming potentially harmful items, buy a pet-proof trash can or keep the trash can in a locked cabinet.

f. *Plants:* Dogs may be poisoned by certain indoor plants. Make sure the plants in your home are safe for your Cavapoo by doing some research on them, and get rid of any dangerous ones.

2. Making a Cavapoo-Safe Zone

It's crucial to have a designated space where your new Cavapoo can feel secure and at home when you bring them home. This area should be safe, distraction-free, and equipped with everything your dog needs to be comfortable. What you'll need for your Cavapoo-safe zone is listed below:

a. *Crate or Playpen:* Your Cavapoo can rest and sleep in a safe, comfortable den in a crate or playpen. Additionally, it will facilitate potty training and offer a safe haven if you must leave your Cavapoo unattended. Make sure the crate is the right size and has a cozy bed or blanket. The pup should be able to stand up straight and be able to turn around comfortably in their crate.

b. *Food and Water Bowls:* To make it simple for your Cavapoo to eat and drink when necessary, put food and water bowls in their safe zone. To avoid spills, look for bowls with non-slip bottoms.

c. *Toys:* Give your Cavapoo a selection of toys to chew on and play with. This will amuse them while also assisting in discouraging destructive chewing behaviors.

d. *Potty Area:* Establish a specific outdoor area, a puppy pad, or an indoor dog toilet as your Cavapoo's designated potty area. As a result, housebreaking will be simpler and more reliable.

3. Establishing Boundaries

Setting boundaries within your home is crucial for keeping things safe and in order. Think about the subsequent techniques for establishing restrictions and boundaries:

a. *Baby gate:* Baby gates are a great way to prevent children from entering certain rooms of your house. Use them to block staircases, rooms with delicate items, or spaces that could be dangerous.

b. *Doors Closed:* Keep the doors to any areas you don't want your Cavapoo to enter closed. This is crucial in places where dangerous chemicals might be kept, like bathrooms and laundry rooms.

c. *Designated Furniture:* Select particular pieces of furniture where your Cavapoo is permitted to relax and play. This will stop your dog from jumping up on expensive or delicate furniture and possibly damaging it.

MAKING A SECURE OUTDOOR AREA

It's crucial to make your Cavapoo's outdoor space, if you have one, safe and enjoyable. Here are some pointers for making a safe outdoor space:

a. *Fencing:* A secure fence around your yard will keep your Cavapoo from getting lost or coming into contact with dangerous wildlife. Look for any openings or weak points in the fence where your dog could escape. Consider adding a barrier along the bottom of the fence if your Cavapoo is particularly skilled at digging in order to discourage digging attempts.

b. *Shelter and Shade:* Give your Cavapoo a comfortable place to rest that is shaded and protected from the elements. A dog house, a covered patio, or sizable trees that provide shade are examples of this.

c. *Water Source:* When your Cavapoo is outdoors, especially in hot weather, make sure there is a clean, fresh water source nearby.

d. *Secure Trash and Compost:* Ensure that your Cavapoo cannot access your outdoor trash and compost bins. Consuming decaying food or trash can result in disease or harm.

e. *Toxic Plants:* Become familiar with any toxic plants that may be in your yard and make sure your Cavapoo cannot access them by either removing them or making sure they are out of reach.

GUIDELINES FOR PUPPY-PROOFING YOUR HOME

There are some special considerations for young dogs that are particularly curious and prone to chewing when it comes to puppy-proofing. Additional advice for dog-proofing your home is provided below:

a. *Furniture Protection:* Use furniture covers or a pet-safe deterrent spray to keep curious puppies from chewing on your furniture. You can encourage your puppy when they choose the chew toy over the furniture by giving them appropriate chew toys.

b. *Stairs:* Puppies may be more likely to trip over them or fall and hurt themselves. To prevent your puppy from accessing stairs until they are more confident and coordinated, think about using baby gates.

c. *Toilet Lid:* Keep the lid closed on the toilet to stop your dog from drinking contaminated water or falling in.

d. *Clothing and Shoes:* Puppies may be drawn to clothing and shoes, especially things that have your scent on them. To avoid them becoming chew toys, keep these items out of the way.

CHANGING AS YOUR CAVAPOO DEVELOPS

Your home may need modifications as your Cavapoo ages and develops new needs and abilities. An older Cavapoo, for instance, might find it challenging to climb stairs because of joint pain or mobility problems. As a result, you might want to think about adding ramps or non-slip stair treads to make it simpler for your dog to navigate the house. As your Cavapoo grows, make sure their safe space is still cozy and convenient, and change their crate's size and bedding as necessary.

SUPPLIES YOU NEED FOR YOUR NEW CAVAPOO

To make your Cavapoo's transition as easy as possible, you'll need to make a safe and comfortable environment as well as a few necessary supplies. The following is a list of some essentials:

1. *Collar and Leash:* For walks and other outdoor activities, your Cavapoo needs a collar and leash. Make sure the collar is cozy and adjustable, and select a dependable leash with enough length for walking.

2. *Identification Tags:* Spend money on an identification tag that includes your contact information, the name of your Cavapoo,

and optionally proof of its rabies vaccination. To ensure that they can be found safely if they ever go missing, attach the tag to their collar.

3. *Bedding:* Give your Cavapoo a cozy bed or blanket to rest on while they sleep in their crate or other designated sleeping space.

4. *Treats:* Keep a supply of dog treats on hand to give your pet as a reward for good behavior, as a teaching tool, or just as a tasty snack.

5. *Grooming Equipment:* Cavapoos need regular grooming to maintain a healthy coat. Get a dog shampoo, nail trimmer, brush, comb, and ear cleaner.

GETTING YOUR CAVAPOO USED TO OTHER ANIMALS

It's crucial to properly introduce your new Cavapoo to any other pets you have in the house if you want to create a peaceful and harmonious atmosphere. To ensure a smooth process, follow these steps:

1. **Prep Well:** Prepare your other pets by giving them a blanket or other item with your new dog's scent on it before bringing your Cavapoo home. This makes the in-person introduction less intimidating and helps them get used to the Cavapoo's smell.

2. **Manage Introductions:** When it's time to meet your pets, do so in a controlled setting with both animals on leashes (if possible) and a helper. Keep the introduction brief and encouraging, rewarding your pets' composure with treats and praise. As they become more at ease with one another, gradually lengthen their interactions.

3. **Separate Spaces:** At first, give your Cavapoo and other pets their own areas to hang out in so that they can get used to each other's presence without being pressured to interact.

4. **Supervision:** Keep an eye on your Cavapoo's interactions with other animals. If you see any aggression or signs of distress, intervene and separate them.

5. **Patience:** Keep in mind that each pet is unique, so it might take some time for your Cavapoo and the other animals in your household to get along. Give them the space and time they require to adjust while being patient.

You can create a secure and welcoming environment for your Cavapoo by adhering to these rules. It's important to keep in mind that as your dog grows and develops, adjustments may be needed to cavapoo-proof your home. You and your new companion will live a happy, healthy life together if you keep an eye out for potential dangers and discover inventive ways to make your Cavapoo's living space better.

CHAPTER 4:
THE FIRST FEW DAYS
AND NIGHTS

The process of bringing your new Cavapoo home can be exciting and enjoyable. As you get used to the new duties and routines that come with pet ownership, it can also be a little overwhelming. We'll talk about how to make your new Cavapoo's first few days and nights with you as easygoing and stress-free as possible in this chapter. We will talk about setting up routines and boundaries, overcoming typical obstacles, and stressing the value of patience and consistency during this exciting transitional phase.

CREATING SCHEDULES AND BOUNDARIES

During the early days of adjusting to your new life together, routines and boundaries are crucial for you and your Cavapoo. By putting these things in place right away, you establish a stable environment that is simpler for your puppy to comprehend and navigate. Here are some guidelines for creating schedules and limits in your home:

1. **Feeding Schedule:** Establish a feeding schedule for your Cavapoo to help control their digestion and make sure they are getting the right nutrition. Establish a specific location for their food and water dishes and follow a regular feeding schedule. While adult dogs may only need to be fed twice daily, puppies should be fed three to four times per day. Choose a high-quality dog food that satisfies your Cavapoo's nutritional needs, and if you have any questions about their dietary requirements, talk to your veterinarian.

2. **Potty Training:** Set up a designated "potty spot" outside and start potty training as soon as possible. Take your Cavapoo to this location consistently in the morning, after meals, and right before bed. When they use the restroom successfully, praise them and give them treats. Be ready for accidents in

the beginning, and keep in mind that the keys to successful potty training are persistence and positive reinforcement. During the early phases of training, the use of puppy pads or a designated indoor potty area can be helpful, especially in case of bad weather or when you are unable to take them outside as frequently as necessary.

3. **Exercise and Play:** Create a daily schedule for exercise and play to keep your Cavapoo active and mentally engaged. Additionally, this will help avoid potential behavioral problems in the future. Regular walks and interactive play with toys and games that are suitable for their size and age should be provided for your Cavapoo. To ensure your Cavapoo's safety while playing, always keep an eye on them.

4. **Sleeping Arrangements:** Choose a location for your Cavapoo to sleep and stick with it. Crate training is a popular choice among owners because it can give your Cavapoo a safe, cozy place to sleep while also helping to establish boundaries. Whether you decide to crate train your Cavapoo or not, you must make sure that it is aware of where their designated sleeping area is in the house. To make your Cavapoo feel safe and at ease, furnish their space with a cozy bed, blankets, and a few toys.

5. **Rules and Boundaries:** Establish clear boundaries for your Cavapoo, such as which rooms or pieces of furniture are off-limits, and consistently enforce them. To achieve this, simply redirect your Cavapoo when they try to enter an area that is off limits and praise them when they do so. Your Cavapoo will eventually come to respect these limitations. When necessary, playpens or baby gates can be used to help maintain these boundaries and keep your Cavapoo safe.

MANAGING COMMON CHALLENGES

As you and your new Cavapoo adjust to your new life together, there may be some difficulties during the first few days and nights. Here are some common problems you might run into and solutions:

1. **Nighttime Crying:** Puppies frequently cry their first few nights in a new home because they may be scared or lonely. Place their sleeping area close to your bedroom so they can feel your presence and it will help them feel less distressed. To simulate the warmth of their littermates, you can also use a plush toy or a warm water bottle wrapped in a blanket. Keep in mind to be patient and realize that your Cavapoo will eventually feel more at ease in their new surroundings. Eventually, as they gain comfort and confidence in their surroundings, you can relocate their sleeping area if needed.

2. **Separation Anxiety:** Due to their affectionate nature, Cavapoos are prone to developing separation anxiety. To help your puppy develop confidence and become more accustomed to your absence, start working on gradually increasing the amount of time they spend alone. To keep them occupied while you're gone, give them engaging toys like chew toys or puzzle feeders. Be mindful of supervising your puppy, especially when there's a choking hazard with snacks or toys. Never punish your Cavapoo for exhibiting symptoms of anxiety; doing so will only make things worse. Instead, concentrate on encouraging them and progressively boosting their independence.

3. **Biting and Mouthing:** Because puppies use their mouths to explore their surroundings, they might start biting and mouthing on various objects, such as your hands and feet. Redirect your Cavapoo to a suitable chew toy and reward

them when they interact with it to stop this behavior. Playing with your hands or feet should be avoided because it might unintentionally encourage biting. Teaching your Cavapoo the commands "leave it" and "drop it" can also be a useful management tool.

4. **Socialization:** It's important to start socializing your Cavapoo young in order to expose them to a variety of people, pets, and environments so they can grow up to be happy, confident, and well-adjusted. As soon as you can, start socializing your Cavapoo by gradually exposing them to new things. Always make sure that these interactions are positive and non-threatening. You can introduce your Cavapoo to other puppies and teach them appropriate play behavior by enrolling them in puppy socialization classes.

THE VALUE OF PERSISTENCE AND PATIENCE

The value of being patient and consistent during the first few days and nights with your Cavapoo cannot be overstated. These characteristics will lay the groundwork for a smooth transition and open the door to a peaceful relationship between you and your new furry friend.

1. **Patience:** Recognize that your Cavapoo is going through a significant environment change and will require some time to adjust. As they become accustomed to your household's customs and procedures, be patient with them and keep in mind that failures are a common part of the learning process. The adjustment process will only become more challenging for you both if you become frustrated or angry with your Cavapoo.

2. **Consistency:** Your Cavapoo will comprehend what is expected of them more quickly if you remain consistent in

your approach to routines, boundaries, and training. Keep to the rules you've established, and make sure everyone in your home is on board with enforcing them. Utilizing the same words and actions when giving commands and when teaching your Cavapoo new skills will aid in their learning.

The first few days and nights you spend with your new Cavapoo may be both exciting and difficult, to sum up. You can make the transition easier on yourself and your Cavapoo by establishing routines and boundaries, dealing with typical problems, and exercising patience and consistency. Keep in mind that while the beginning may be difficult for you both, with time, love, and commitment, you will build a solid relationship and a fulfilling life together.

CHAPTER 5:

BONDING WITH YOUR CAVAPOO

Developing a strong bond with your Cavapoo, creating trust and attachment, the value of play in fostering that bond, and appropriate socialization with other dogs and people are all topics we'll cover in this chapter. A harmonious and fulfilling relationship with your Cavapoo depends on you two having a strong bond. It makes it simpler to train and take care of your dog because it helps you better understand their needs and behaviors.

GROWING ATTACHMENT AND TRUST

The gradual process of developing trust and attachment with your Cavapoo starts the moment you bring your new furry family member home. Establishing trust is crucial because it will lay the groundwork for a long-lasting, satisfying relationship. You can help your Cavapoo develop trust and attachment by using the following techniques.

CALM AND KIND APPROACH

Your Cavapoo might be fearful or timid when you first bring them home because of their unfamiliar surroundings. Approach them in a calm, gentle manner to ease their transition and prevent scaring them. Send a message of comfort and security by speaking softly and acting in a positive way with your body.

ROUTINE AND CONSISTENCY

Your Cavapoo will feel more secure and predictable if you establish a routine for them. Feed, walk, and play with them at regular intervals throughout the day. As they learn to rely on you to meet their needs, this consistency helps develop trust.

POSITIVE REINFORCEMENT

Building attachment and trust can be accomplished by using positive reinforcement. When your Cavapoo behaves well, such as by sitting or responding when called, praise and reward them. This will help strengthen your dog's attachment to you and motivate them to continue acting in this way.

BASIC NEEDS OF YOUR CAVAPOO

Ensure that your Cavapoo has access to food, water, shelter, and exercise. By meeting their needs, you earn their trust and demonstrate to them your commitment to their welfare.

PATIENCE

It takes time to develop trust and attachment, so your Cavapoo might be wary or anxious at first. To help them feel more at ease in their new surroundings, be patient and give them space when necessary.

THE BENEFITS OF PLAY FOR BOND STRENGTHENING

Play is a crucial part of building a relationship with your Cavapoo. Playing with your dog stimulates his mind and body while also aiding in the development of attachment and trust. Make sure your Cavapoo gets a variety of types of playtime each day to keep him or her happy, healthy, and interested.

VARIOUS TYPES OF PLAY

There are many different types of play that can help you and your Cavapoo become closer. These consist of:

— **Tug-of-war:** This age-old game entails pulling on opposite ends of a toy with your dog. This activity can help you gain strength and give your Cavapoo a constructive outlet for their natural instincts.

— **Fetch:** To keep your Cavapoo active and interested, throw a ball or toy for them to retrieve. Additionally strengthening your bond, this game teaches your dog to obey your commands.

— **Hide and Seek:** Play hide and seek with your Cavapoo. Hide treats or toys around your house or yard, and encourage him to use his nose to find them. Playing this game helps to strengthen your relationship with your dog while also stimulating your mind.

— **Puzzle toys:** These toys require your Cavapoo to solve puzzles in order to access treats that are hidden inside. Puzzle toys can amuse your dog and strengthen your relationship as you solve the puzzles together.

CREATING LIMITS AND BOUNDARIES

Even though playing together is a crucial part of bonding, it's important to set limits to keep playtime safe and enjoyable. To avoid possessiveness or aggression during play, teach your Cavapoo to pay attention to commands like "drop it" or "leave it."

PROPER SOCIALIZATION OF YOUR DOG WITH PEOPLE & OTHER DOGS

Building a well-rounded and content dog requires socializing your Cavapoo with both people and other dogs. You can help your Cavapoo gain confidence and learn how to adjust to various situations by exposing them to a variety of environments, people, and animals.

TIPS FOR SOCIALIZATION

You can successfully socialize your Cavapoo by using the advice below:

- **Start socialization early:** Puppies should be socialized between the ages of 3 and 14 weeks. It is crucial to expose your Cavapoo to various people, animals, and environments during this period.

- **Employ positive reinforcement:** Reward your Cavapoo when they behave calmly and amicably in social situations by giving them treats, compliments, and love. They will be inspired to keep interacting well with others by this.

- **Gradual exposure:** To prevent overwhelming your Cavapoo, introduce new situations and experiences to them gradually. As your dog becomes more comfortable, gradually lengthen the interactions and intensify them. Begin with brief, controlled interactions.

- **Enroll in puppy socialization classes:** In a safe setting, puppy classes are a great way to introduce your Cavapoo to other dogs and people. Look for courses being offered by local pet shops or expert dog trainers.

- **Visit dog-friendly places:** To help your Cavapoo get used to interacting with other dogs and people, take them frequently to dog parks, pet stores, and other dog-friendly places.

- **Car rides:** To make sure your Cavapoo feels safe and secure when traveling, get them used to them as early as possible. Regular car trips can also offer more chances to experience new environments and things.

THE VALUE OF CONTINUOUS SOCIALIZATION

It's important to continually expose your Cavapoo to new experiences throughout their life because socialization is not a one-time thing. Regular social interactions will keep your Cavapoo adaptable and at ease in a variety of situations by preventing fear, aggression, or shyness.

In conclusion, developing a bond with your Cavapoo is a continuous process that calls for tolerance, reliability, and commitment. You can create a solid, enduring bond with your Cavapoo by paying attention to the advice provided in this chapter, which will ultimately result in a joyful and rewarding relationship.

CHAPTER 6:
NUTRITION AND
FEEDING

In this section, we'll discuss the Cavapoo's dietary requirements and how to make sure they get the nutrition they need all their lives. This chapter will give you the information and assurance to choose the right foods for your Cavapoo's diet, as well as how to deal with food allergies and sensitivities.

THE BENEFITS OF HEALTHY NUTRITION

Understanding the significance of giving your Cavapoo a healthy, balanced diet is crucial before delving into the various aspects of Cavapoo nutrition. For the overall health and wellbeing of your Cavapoo, proper nutrition is essential. A diet that satisfies their nutritional requirements will give them the energy they require for an active, happy life, support their immune system, help them maintain a healthy weight, and promote good dental health.

RECOGNIZING CAVAPOO DIETARY REQUIREMENTS

You must feed your Cavapoo puppy a diet that satisfies their particular nutritional needs as a parent. Since the Cavapoo is a hybrid of the Cavalier King Charles Spaniel and the Poodle, it possesses characteristics of both breeds. When it comes to nutrition, it's important to take into account the distinct dietary requirements of each parent breed as well as any potential health problems that Cavapoos might experience.

The average weight of a Cavapoo is between 12 and 25 pounds (5.4 and 11.3 kilograms), making them small to medium-sized dogs. Depending on their size, age, and level of activity, they will have different energy needs. Cavapoos typically require 40 calories per pound of body weight. For instance, a 15-pound (6.8-kg) Cavapoo might need about 600 calories per day. This is only a general recommendation, so it's important to keep an eye on your Cavapoo's weight and modify their daily caloric intake as necessary.

For the macronutrient makeup of a Cavapoo's diet, a balance of superior proteins, fats, and carbohydrates is needed. In contrast to fats, which offer a concentrated source of energy and essential fatty acids for healthy skin and fur, protein is crucial for the growth of muscles and for overall development. The best sources of carbohydrates are those that are high-quality and simple to digest.

Take into account the following general recommendations when selecting a diet for your Cavapoo:

1. **Protein:** Aim for at least 18 to 22 percent of your diet to come from animal sources like chicken, turkey, fish, or beef.

2. **Fat:** Cavapoos should generally consume a diet that is 14–18% fat, with an emphasis on consuming healthy fats from sources like fish, flaxseed, and other foods high in omega-3 and omega-6 fatty acids.

3. **Carbohydrates:** Look for complex carbohydrates, which include whole grains, vegetables, and fruits. These foods also contain dietary fiber, essential vitamins, and minerals.

4. **Vitamins and Minerals:** Ensure that your Cavapoo eats a balanced diet that is full of the vitamins and minerals it needs to maintain good health overall.

CHOOSING THE CORRECT DIET AND FEEDING ROUTINE

It's time to select the ideal food for your dog now that you are familiar with the fundamentals of Cavapoo nutrition. When deciding on the ideal diet for your Cavapoo, there are a number of things to take into account:

1. **Age:** Cavapoos have various nutritional requirements throughout their lives. While adult dogs need a diet that maintains their general health and prevents weight gain, puppies need a diet that supports their rapid growth and development. A senior Cavapoo's diet may be necessary to address age-related health issues.

2. **Activity Level:** While less active dogs will need fewer calories to maintain a healthy weight, highly active Cavapoos may need a diet with a higher calorie content to support their energy needs.

3. **Medical and Health Conditions:** A change in diet may be necessary to manage the symptoms of some medical conditions, such as allergies or digestive problems, and to enhance general health.

4. **Food Quality:** Select premium dog food that is made with all-natural ingredients and few additives. Real meat should be the first ingredient on the ingredient list, and a variety of whole foods should also be present to supply necessary vitamins and minerals.

After selecting the ideal food for your Cavapoo, create a regular feeding schedule. While adult dogs can only eat two meals per day, one in the morning and one in the evening, puppies should be fed three to four times daily. To ensure accurate portion sizes and avoid overfeeding, measure the food you give your Cavapoo using a measuring cup or scale.

ADDRESSING FOOD SENSITIVITIES AND ALLERGIES

Food sensitivities and allergies are common in Cavapoos, and they can result in a variety of symptoms, such as ear infections, skin rashes, and digestive issues. It is essential to speak with your veterinarian if you think your Cavapoo might be allergic to or sensitive to certain foods in order to identify the problem and create a treatment plan for the symptoms.

In some circumstances, altering your Cavapoo's diet may be required to locate and get rid of the allergens that are bothering him. Under the direction of your veterinarian, this might entail switching to a diet with fewer ingredients, one with a novel protein source, or one that is hypoallergenic.

MONITORING AND MODIFYING YOUR CAVAPOO'S DIET

It's critical to keep an eye on your Cavapoo's weight and general health to make sure their diet is providing all the nutrients they require. You can spot any changes in your Cavapoo's health that might require a diet adjustment by performing routine body condition checks and weigh-ins.

To decide the best course of action if your Cavapoo is gaining or losing weight, speak with your veterinarian. To reach and maintain a healthy weight, they might advise modifying your Cavapoo's diet, increasing their daily exercise, or adjusting their caloric intake.

In conclusion, a crucial aspect of your Cavapoo's overall health and wellbeing is proper nutrition. You can make sure that your cherished Cavapoo lives a long, fulfilling, and healthy life by being aware of their particular dietary needs, choosing high-quality food, and keeping an eye on their weight and physical condition.

CHAPTER 7:
HEALTH AND
WELLNESS

The various health and wellness issues that Cavapoo owners should be aware of are covered in this chapter. We'll go over everything you need to know to keep your Cavapoo happy and healthy for the duration of their life, from common health issues to the significance of routine veterinary care, vaccinations, and spaying/neutering.

CAVAPOOS' COMMON HEALTH PROBLEMS

The Cavalier King Charles Spaniel and the Poodle are the parent breeds of the Cavapoo, which is a mixed breed. Overall, this may make the dog healthier and more robust, but Cavapoos may still be more prone to certain health problems. Knowing about these potential health issues can make it easier for you to support your dog's overall wellbeing and deal with any problems that may develop.

1. **Hip Dysplasia:** This genetic condition causes arthritis and pain in the hip joint because the hip joint doesn't develop properly. Larger dog breeds are more frequently affected by hip dysplasia, but smaller breeds like Cavapoos are also susceptible. Hip dysplasia symptoms can be avoided or reduced with regular exercise and maintaining a healthy weight.

2. **Patellar Luxation:** Also referred to as "slipped kneecaps," patellar luxation happens when the kneecap slips out of place. Small dogs with this common condition may experience pain and have trouble walking. Surgery might be required in some circumstances to resolve the problem.

3. **Eye Issues:** Cataracts, progressive retinal atrophy (PRA), and dry eyes are just a few of the eye conditions that Cavapoos are susceptible to. Your dog's regular eye exams by your veterinarian can help identify these issues early and guarantee that it receives the right care.

4. **Heart Problems:** Heart issues, such as mitral valve disease, which can result in heart failure, can affect both Cavalier King Charles Spaniels and Poodles. Regular vet visits that include listening to the heart of your dog can aid in spotting any potential problems early on.

5. **Ear Infections:** Cavapoos are more susceptible to ear infections than some other breeds because of their floppy ears. Cleaning and drying your dog's ears can help ward off infections.

6. **Allergies:** Cavapoos, like people, can develop allergies. Itching, redness, and other skin irritations are possible symptoms. Your veterinarian can suggest the best courses of action for treating the allergy and determining its root cause.

7. **Digestive Problems:** Some Cavapoos may have digestive problems, including inflammatory bowel disease or food sensitivities. Consult your veterinarian to identify the cause and the best course of action if you experience any signs of digestive issues, such as vomiting or diarrhea.

8. **Dental Issues:** Cavapoos are susceptible to dental problems like plaque accumulation, gum disease, and tooth decay. Regular dental care, such as tooth brushing and giving dental chews to your dog, can help to prevent these issues.

Even though this list may seem overwhelming, it's important to keep in mind that most Cavapoos will experience healthy lives free from these ailments. Regular veterinary care and preventative measures can greatly contribute to the health of your Cavapoo.

ROUTINE VACCINATIONS AND VETERINARY CARE

Making sure your Cavapoo receives routine veterinary care is one of the fundamental facets of responsible dog ownership. This includes scheduling routine check-ups, vaccinations, and preventative treatments in addition to just taking your dog to the vet when they're sick.

1. **Annual Checkups:** Dogs should receive regular checkups to monitor their general health, just like people do. Your Cavapoo's ears, eyes, teeth, heart, and other organs will all be checked during a comprehensive physical examination by your veterinarian at least once a year. This is a great chance to talk about any worries you might have and get tailored advice for the needs of your dog.

2. **Vaccinations:** Vaccinating your Cavapoo is essential for defending them against diseases that could be fatal. Vaccinations against rabies, parvovirus, hepatitis, and distemper are typically included in the vaccination schedule. Based on your dog's age and lifestyle, your veterinarian will be able to give you a recommended vaccination schedule.

3. **Heartworm, Flea, and Tick Prevention:** Regular preventative treatments are necessary to keep your Cavapoo free of parasites. Mosquitoes can carry the potentially fatal disease heartworm, so it's essential to make sure your dog takes a regular heartworm preventative. Oral or topical flea and tick prevention medications can help keep your dog free of these bothersome and disease-carrying pests.

4. **Fecal Examinations and Deworming:** Dogs can experience a variety of health issues as a result of intestinal parasites like roundworms, hookworms, and tapeworms. Regular fecal examinations (at least once a year) can help spot any problems,

and if deworming treatments are required, your veterinarian can advise you on them.

5. **Blood Tests:** As your Cavapoo ages, your veterinarian may advise blood tests to track their general health and spot any potential problems before they become serious. Blood tests can aid in the early detection of conditions like diabetes, kidney disease, and liver disease.

THE VALUE OF DENTAL CARE & SPAYING/NEUTERING

Spaying/neutering and dental care are two essential components of maintaining the health of your Cavapoo in addition to routine veterinary exams and vaccinations.

SPAYING/NEUTERING:

For your Cavapoo, spaying (for female dogs) or neutering (for male dogs) has a number of behavioral and health benefits. In order to prevent your dog from reproducing and adding to the pet overpopulation, these procedures involve removing the reproductive organs.

1. **Health Advantages:** Having your Cavapoo spayed or neutered can help to avoid a number of health problems. While neutering male dogs can prevent testicular cancer and lower the risk of prostate issues, spaying female dogs can help to prevent uterine infections and breast cancer.

2. **Behavioral Benefits:** Spaying or neutering your Cavapoo has behavioral advantages in addition to health advantages. Males who have been neutered are less likely to mark their territory, stray from their homes, and act aggressively. Females who have been spayed will not go into heat, which can be difficult for both the dog and the owner.

3. **When to Spay/Neuter:** The ideal age to spay or neuter your Cavapoo can vary depending on their size, breed, and general health, among other things. It is typically advised to spay or neuter your dog between the ages of 6 and 9 months. Some vets, especially those who specialize in male dogs, might advise waiting until your dog is a little older. To find out when is best for your Cavapoo, speak with your vet.

DENTAL TREATMENT:

An important part of your Cavapoo's overall wellbeing is maintaining their dental health. Plaque accumulation, gum disease, tooth decay, and even more serious health issues can result from neglecting dental care.

1. **Regular Brushing:** Brushing your dog's teeth on a regular basis is one of the best ways to maintain their dental health. Aim to use a toothbrush and toothpaste made for dogs to brush your Cavapoo's teeth at least a few times per week.

2. **Dental Chews and Toys:** Providing dental chews and toys to your Cavapoo can help to stimulate their gums and lessen plaque buildup. Always keep an eye on your dog while they are chewing, and look for chews and toys that are intended to promote dental health.

3. **Professional Cleanings:** Your veterinarian might advise professional dental cleanings depending on the state of your dog's teeth. These under-anesthesia cleanings enable a complete examination of your dog's teeth and the elimination of any plaque or tartar accumulation.

You can contribute to ensuring that your Cavapoo lives a long, happy, and healthy life by your side by spending time and energy on their health and wellness.

CHAPTER 8:
GROOMING AND
MAINTENANCE

A crucial part of providing for your Cavapoo is grooming. Regular grooming helps maintain your dog's general health and well-being in addition to keeping them looking their best. We will go over how often to perform basic grooming tasks, how to properly bathe and brush your Cavapoo, as well as other important grooming chores like nail trimming, ear cleaning, and dental care in this chapter.

TASKS & FREQUENCY FOR BASIC GROOMING

Due to their curly or wavy coats, Cavapoos require routine grooming in order to maintain their best appearance and health. Depending on the type of coat your Cavapoo has, their particular grooming requirements may change, but there are a few fundamental tasks that every Cavapoo owner should be prepared to perform on a regular basis.

1. **Brushing:** Regular brushing is essential to maintaining the health and tangle-free coat of your Cavapoo. If your Cavapoo has a curly or thick coat, aim to brush them more frequently— at least four times per week. Regular brushing helps to distribute natural oils throughout the coat, remove loose hair, and prevent mats and tangles.

2. **Bathing:** They might require frequent baths, but bathing is necessary to keep a Cavapoo's coat clean and free of dirt and debris. Aim to give your Cavapoo a bath every four to six weeks, or more frequently if necessary, depending on how much they are active and how clean their coat is.

3. **Nail Trimming:** Your Cavapoo's comfort and general health depend on you keeping their nails trimmed. Long nails can be uncomfortable and may make it difficult to run, jump, or walk. Depending on how fast they grow, aim to trim your Cavapoo's nails every three to four weeks.

4. **Ear Cleaning:** Cavapoos' floppy ears make them vulnerable to ear infections. Regular ear cleaning can keep your dog's ears healthy and help prevent infections. Aim to clean your Cavapoo's ears once every two to three weeks, or more frequently if wax and debris accumulate.

5. **Brushing Teeth:** As was mentioned in the previous chapter, maintaining your Cavapoo's dental health is crucial for their general wellbeing. To prevent plaque buildup and maintain good oral hygiene, try to brush your Cavapoo's teeth at least two to three times per week.

HOW TO BATHE AND GROOM YOUR CAVAPOO CORRECTLY

After discussing the necessary grooming procedures and how frequently they should be performed, let's go into greater detail about how to properly bathe and brush your Cavapoo.

HOW TO BATHE A CAVAPOO

1. **Gather Supplies:** Before you start, gather all the bathing necessities. This includes a towel, a non-slip bath mat, a brush or comb, dog-safe shampoo, and treats for rewarding your dog.

2. **Brush Before the Bath:** to make the bathing process simpler and more effective. This will make it simpler to thoroughly clean their coat by removing any tangles and loose hair.

3. **Protect the Ears:** Optionally insert cotton balls into each ear canal to stop water from entering your Cavapoo's ears while it is bathing. After the bath, make sure to take them out

4. **Thoroughly Wet the Coat:** Wet your dog's coat with lukewarm water. Be careful not to get water in their eyes or ears.

5. **Shampoo:** Wash your Cavapoo with a dog-safe shampoo, working your way down from the neck to the body. Make sure to thoroughly clean all areas, including the legs, chest, and belly, by gently massaging the shampoo into the coat.

6. **Rinse:** Make sure all shampoo is removed from your Cavapoo's coat by giving them a good rinse in lukewarm water. To avoid irritating the dog, take extra care around the eyes and ears.

7. **Apply Conditioner:** To keep your Cavapoo's coat soft and manageable if it has a curly or thick coat, you may want to use a conditioner safe for dogs. After applying the conditioner as directed, thoroughly rinse your hair.

8. **Dry:** Towel-dry your Cavapoo gently, being careful not to rub their coat too hard or cause tangles. If your Cavapoo is tolerant of it, you can also hasten the drying process by using a hairdryer on the lowest heat setting. To prevent burning your dog's skin, keep the hairdryer at a safe distance and pay attention to the heat.

9. **Reward:** To reinforce the positive experience, give your Cavapoo praise and treats after the bath.

BRUSHING YOUR CAVAPOO:

1. **Pick the Right Brush:** Depending on the coat type of your Cavapoo, choose an appropriate brush or comb. A slicker brush or a pin brush works best on wavy coats, whereas a comb or rake may be more effective on curly coats.

2. **Brush in Sections:** Working your way down the body, begin at the head and neck region and brush in small sections. Concentrate on one area at a time, making sure to brush the entire coat to get rid of any loose hair and avoid tangles.

3. **Be Gentle:** Be gentle when brushing your Cavapoo to prevent any pain. Before attempting to brush through a tangle or mat, gently separate the hair with your fingers. Additionally, using a detangling spray can facilitate the process.

4. **Reward:** To reinforce the positive experience, give your Cavapoo praise and treats after brushing.

TRIMMING NAILS, CLEANING EARS AND DENTAL CARE

Owners of Cavapoos should be prepared to perform additional necessary grooming tasks on a regular basis in addition to bathing and brushing their pets. Let's look more closely at each of these assignments.

TRIMMING NAILS

1. **Pick the Right Tool:** Depending on the size and thickness of your Cavapoo's nails, choose a nail trimmer. Both guillotine-style and scissor-style trimmers are acceptable choices.

2. **Trim in a Calm Environment:** Pick a peaceful, well-lit area for nail trimming in order to keep your dog calm and to make it easier for you to see the nails.

3. **Securely Hold Your Cavapoo:** With one hand supporting your Cavapoo's body and the other holding the nail trimmer, you can safely hold your Cavapoo in your lap or on a table.

4. **Locate the Quick:** The quick is the blood vessel that runs through the nail. Find it before trimming. Usually, the quick can be seen as a darker area close to the nail's base. Avoid cutting into the quick because doing so can hurt and result in bleeding.

5. **Trim the Nail:** Make a 45-degree angle cut just above the quick with the nail trimmer. Start with small cuts if you are unsure of how much to trim to avoid slicing into the quick.

6. **Reward:** To make the experience rewarding, give your Cavapoo praise and treats after trimming.

CLEANING THE EARS

1. **Pick the Right Cleaner:** Choose an ear cleaning solution safe for dogs, which is available from your veterinarian or at pet stores.

2. **Soak a Cotton Ball:** After soaking the cotton ball in the ear cleaning solution, gently squeeze out any extra liquid.

3. **Clean the Ear:** Using a cotton ball, gently wipe your Cavapoo's outer ear to get rid of any dirt, debris, or wax buildup. A cotton ball or your fingers should not be inserted into the ear canal as this could result in damage.

4. **Dry the Ear:** After cleaning, gently dry the ear using a clean, dry cotton ball.

5. **Reward:** To reinforce the positive experience, give your Cavapoo praise and treats after the ear cleaning.

DENTAL HYGIENE:

For thorough instructions on how to brush your Cavapoo's teeth and preserve their dental health, see Chapter 7.

Your Cavapoo will look and feel their best if you keep up a consistent grooming schedule, which will also benefit their general health and wellbeing. In addition to being important for your dog's physical well-being, grooming gives you and your Cavapoo the chance to connect and strengthen your relationship.

CHAPTER 9:

TRAINING YOUR CAVAPOO

Intelligent and eager to please, Cavapoos are renowned for their quick learning abilities. To raise a Cavapoo who is content and well-adjusted, training is crucial. The most important commands for obedience will be covered in this chapter, along with positive reinforcement training methods and how to deal with behavioral problems like jumping, barking, and chewing.

ESSENTIAL COMMANDS FOR OBEDIENCE: A DETAILED GUIDE

Training your Cavapoo is an essential part of responsible pet ownership. Teaching these fundamental commands will not only help your Cavapoo become well-mannered and confident but also strengthen the bond between you and your pet. Here's a more in-depth guide on how to train your Cavapoo these 7 essential commands.

1. Sit

The 'Sit' command is one of the simplest and most useful commands your Cavapoo can learn. It's a great command for helping to calm an excited or nervous dog.

- Start by holding a treat in your closed hand. Make sure your Cavapoo knows it's there but cannot get to it.
- Stand or sit in front of your Cavapoo, holding the treat near their nose to get their attention.
- Slowly raise the treat above your Cavapoo's head. As their head follows the treat, their bottom should naturally move into a sitting position.
- As soon as their bottom hits the ground, say "Sit," give them the treat, and give them plenty of praise.

– Repeat this process multiple times. Always use the same word, and make sure to reward your Cavapoo immediately after they sit.

2. Stay

The 'Stay' command is essential for keeping your Cavapoo safe. It allows you to control your dog in potentially dangerous situations, like near traffic or when you're opening the front door.

– Begin with your Cavapoo in a 'Sit' position. Hold your palm flat towards their face and say "Stay."
– Take a step back. If they stay put, return to them, give them a treat, and lots of praise. If they move, calmly say "No," put them back in the sit position and try again.
– Gradually increase the distance between you and your Cavapoo, rewarding them every time they stay put. This process may take several training sessions, so be patient.

3. Come

The 'Come' command is a vital recall command that can keep your Cavapoo safe in dangerous situations.

– Start with your Cavapoo on a leash. Squat down to their level and say "Come" while gently pulling on the leash.
– As soon as they come to you, reward them with a treat and lots of praise.
– Practice this command in a safe, enclosed area. As your Cavapoo gets better at this command, you can increase the distance and try it off-leash in a secure area.

4. Down

The 'Down' command can be a bit challenging for some dogs to learn, but it's an important one, especially in situations where 'Sit' is not enough.

- Find a particularly good-smelling treat, and hold it in your closed fist.
- Hold your fist close to your Cavapoo's snout. Once they've caught the scent, lower your hand to the floor so they follow.
- Slide your hand along the ground, leading them into a lying down position.
- As soon as they're lying down, say "Down," give them the treat, and share lots of praise.
- Repeat this process multiple times daily. It may take a few days or weeks for your Cavapoo to reliably respond to the 'Down' command, so be patient.

5. Heel

The 'Heel' command is useful for walks, keeping your Cavapoo close and preventing them from pulling on the leash.

- With your Cavapoo sitting to your left, hold a treat in your left hand and let them sniff it.
- Say "Heel," take a step forward. If they follow you and stay by your side, give them the treat and lots of praise.
- If they pull ahead or lag behind, stop and guide them back to your side with a gentle tug on the leash.
- Repeat the command "Heel," and continue walking. Remember, this command requires patience and consistency, and it's important to reward your Cavapoo for walking nicely at your side.

6. Leave It

The 'Leave It' command is important to prevent your Cavapoo from picking up potentially dangerous items.

– Start with a treat in both hands. Close one fist around a less appealing treat, and the other around a more appealing treat.

– Show your Cavapoo the closed fist with the less appealing treat, and say "Leave it."

– Your Cavapoo will likely try to get the treat, sniffing, pawing, and possibly barking. Ignore these behaviors.

– Once your Cavapoo stops trying to get the treat, reward them with the more appealing treat from your other hand.

– Practice this command regularly, increasing the appeal of the 'leave it' treat as your Cavapoo gets better at the command.

7. Off

The 'Off' command can be useful to stop your Cavapoo from jumping on people or furniture.

– Start when your Cavapoo decides to jump on the couch or a person. Firmly say "Off."

– If they get off, reward them with a treat and praise. If they don't, gently guide them off.

– Once they are off, ask them to sit or lay down, then reward them. This helps reinforce a positive behavior in place of the negative one.

– Be consistent with this command and use it every time they jump up.

Remember, training your Cavapoo should be a fun and rewarding experience for both of you. Always use positive reinforcement methods, and never punish your Cavapoo for getting things wrong. It's important to be patient and consistent, and with time, your Cavapoo will start to understand and follow these essential commands.

The Cavapoo must master these fundamental commands in order to be well-trained. You can ensure a contented, obedient, and well-adjusted dog by consistently teaching and reinforcing these commands throughout your dog's life.

TECHNIQUES FOR POSITIVE REINFORCEMENT IN TRAINING

Your Cavapoo will learn which behaviors result in praise, treats, or other rewards through positive reinforcement training, which involves rewarding them for desired behaviors. As it promotes a positive relationship between the dog and the trainer, this method has been demonstrated to be a highly effective and humane way to train dogs. When training your Cavapoo, keep in mind the following important positive reinforcement training principles:

1. **Timing:** For positive reinforcement training, reward timing is essential. Rewarding your Cavapoo right away after they exhibit the desired behavior will help them link the behavior to the reward.

2. **Consistency:** When training your Cavapoo, consistency is essential. Every time you train, make sure to use the same commands and rewards; this will help your dog understand what is expected of them.

3. **Patience:** Keep in mind that each dog learns at their own pace and that training takes time. Encourage and support your Cavapoo patiently as you work through the training process.

4. **Gradual Progression:** Start with simple instructions and work your way up to more complicated ones. With this methodical

approach, you can help your Cavapoo develop their self-assurance and skills.

5. **Quick Sessions:** Keep workouts brief, aiming for 10-15 minutes per session. This keeps your Cavapoo's attention and makes sure that the training is fun and interesting.

6. **Frequency:** Your Cavapoo's routine should include training on a regular basis. For learning to be reinforced and consistency to be maintained, try to train at least a few times per week, ideally every day.

7. **Reward Variety:** To keep your Cavapoo motivated and engaged during training, switch up the rewards you give. Toys, praise, treats, and playtime are examples of this.

By using these positive reinforcement training methods, you can develop a close relationship with your Cavapoo while imparting important knowledge and behaviors.

ADDRESSING BEHAVIORAL ISSUES

Like all dogs, Cavapoos occasionally display some undesirable behaviors. You can assist your Cavapoo in developing into a well-mannered and content pet by identifying the underlying causes of these behaviors and taking the necessary steps to address them.

1. **Jumping:** To get attention or to show excitement, Cavapoos may jump on people or furniture. Teach your dog the "off" command, and reinforce it repeatedly, to stop this behavior. Reward your Cavapoo for remaining calm when greeting strangers and keeping all four paws on the ground.

2. **Barking:** Dogs use their barking as a natural form of communication, but too much barking can be annoying. Find out why your Cavapoo is barking, such as whether it is out of

boredom, fear, or territorial behavior. Deal with the underlying problem and reinforce quiet behavior with praise and rewards.

3. **Chewing:** Chewing is a natural behavior for dogs, but if your Cavapoo chews on inappropriate objects, it can be problematic. Use the "leave it" command to steer your Cavapoo away from inappropriate objects and give them appropriate chew toys. Make sure to reward them when they chew on the proper toys.

You can assist your Cavapoo in developing into a well-behaved and pleasurable companion by comprehending and treating behavioral issues with understanding and persistence.

To sum up, training is a crucial component of raising a contented, well-adjusted Cavapoo. You can develop a close bond with your Cavapoo and make sure that you and your pet get along by teaching them the fundamentals of obedience, using positive reinforcement techniques, and dealing with any behavioral problems. You should be ready to reinforce these abilities and behaviors throughout your Cavapoo's lifetime because training is a continuous process.

CHAPTER 10:

EXERCISE AND MENTAL STIMULATION

Exercise and mental stimulation are essential for your Cavapoo's general health. Regular exercise can promote cardiovascular health, maintain healthy joints, and fight obesity. It prevents boredom, keeps your dog's mind active, and gives them a way to express their innate instincts. This chapter will cover giving your Cavapoo the exercise they require, having fun with them, and stimulating their minds with puzzle toys and training.

MEETING THE EXERCISE NEEDS OF YOUR CAVAPOO

Because they are a moderately active breed, Cavapoos need regular exercise to stay healthy and content. They can adjust to a variety of living arrangements, but regular physical activity should always come first. The following advice will help you fulfill your Cavapoo's exercise requirements:

1. **Daily Walks:** Try to take your Cavapoo for at least one, and ideally two or three, daily walks. The length of walks should be around 30 minutes, with consideration for your dog's age and level of fitness. Remember that younger dogs and older dogs might benefit from shorter walks. Walking has many health advantages, but it also promotes social interaction and mental stimulation by exposing one to new sights and smells.

2. **Playtime:** Make time to play with your Cavapoo on a regular basis to help with calorie burning, mental stimulation, and bonding. Simple forms of play include indoor tug-of-war with their favorite toy and backyard games of fetch.

3. **Dog Parks:** If your Cavapoo is well-mannered and sociable with other dogs, dog parks can be a wonderful place for exercise and off-leash play. At the park, keep an eye on your

dog to make sure they are playing nicely with other dogs and obeying your commands.

4. **Swimming:** A lot of Cavapoos like to swim, and it can be a great low-impact exercise choice, especially for dogs with joint problems or those who get hot easily. Introduce your Cavapoo to the water gradually, and make sure they are always closely watched while swimming.

5. **Hiking and Outdoor Activities:** Your Cavapoo may be a willing travel companion for hiking, camping, or other outdoor adventures if you enjoy being outside. As your Cavapoo's fitness level rises, start with short, easy hikes and gradually increase the difficulty. Have the essentials on hand, such as water, bags for dog waste, and a collapsible bowl for food or water.

6. **Agility and Sports:** Some Cavapoos might take pleasure in competing in agility or other canine sports like flyball or rally obedience. These pursuits can stimulate your dog's body and mind while fostering a closer relationship between you two through cooperative effort.

7. **Adapting Exercise for Age and Health:** You may need to modify your Cavapoo's exercise regimen as they get older or develop health problems. Keep in mind that puppies' joints and bones are still growing, so they shouldn't be overworked. Senior dogs might need slower paces and lower impact activities. For advice on the best type of exercise to give your Cavapoo, always consult your veterinarian.

GAMES AND ACTIVITIES TO
TRY WITH YOUR CAVAPOO

Engaging your Cavapoo in enjoyable activities and games can help them get the additional physical and mental stimulation they need in addition to meeting their basic exercise needs. Here are some suggestions for entertaining and exercising your Cavapoo:

1. **Fetch:** Play fetch with a ball, a frisbee, or your Cavapoo's preferred toy. This age-old game offers a wonderful chance for exercise and camaraderie.

2. **Hide and Seek:** Hide treats or toys around your house or yard and play hide and seek with your Cavapoo. With this game, you can train your dog to use their keen nose and analytical skills.

3. **Tug-of-War:** Use a strong rope toy or other suitable object to play a friendly game of tug-of-war with your Cavapoo. This game gives your dog a physical workout and satisfies his or her innate urge to pull and tug.

4. **Obstacle Course:** Using objects from around the house or natural obstructions, make your Cavapoo a homemade obstacle course. Encourage your dog to navigate the course and give them a treat after they complete each obstacle.

5. **Bubble-chasing:** Some canines, such as Cavapoos, take pleasure in pursuing and popping bubbles. You can encourage your Cavapoo to chase and catch bubbles as they float through the air by purchasing dog-safe bubbles from a pet store.

6. **Find the Treat:** Hide a treat under one of several cups or tiny containers. Then, move the cups around and entice your Cavapoo to discover the treat. This game tests your dog's capacity for problem-solving and stimulates the mind.

7. **Indoor Dog Parkour:** Inspire your Cavapoo to partake in "dog parkour" by posing obstacles inside, like jumping over a broomstick or weaving through a row of chairs. While helping to enhance your dog's balance and coordination, this activity provides both physical exercise and mental stimulation.

Always keep an eye on your Cavapoo when they are playing to ensure their safety and welfare. To keep your dog interested and engaged, switch up the games and activities frequently.

PROMOTING MENTAL EXERCISE WITH PUZZLE TOYS AND PRACTICE

For the overall health of your Cavapoo, mental exercise is crucial. A dog that is mentally stimulated is less likely to act destructively or become bored and lethargic. Here are some strategies for keeping your Cavapoo mentally active:

1. **Puzzle Toys:** There are many puzzle toys on the market made to test your dog's ability to solve puzzles. These toys frequently contain treats or kibble that must be accessed by your dog manipulating the toy in a particular way. These toys can be a great way to stimulate the mind and appeal to the instincts of your Cavapoo.

2. **Interactive Feeding:** Take into account integrating interactive feeding techniques into your Cavapoo's mealtime routine, such as slow feeders or toys that dispense treats. These feeders make your dog work for their food, which stimulates their mind and slows down eating.

3. **Trick Training:** Teaching your Cavapoo new tricks can be a fun and interesting way to stimulate their minds, reinforce their obedience, and deepen your relationship. Begin by learning

basic tricks like "shake" or "roll over," then gradually advance to more difficult ones like "play dead" or "fetch a specific toy."

4. **Nose Work:** Involve your Cavapoo in activities that will help them use their keen sense of smell. This can entail taking part in formal scent work classes or competitions, hiding treats or fragrant objects around your house or yard, or both.

5. **Brain Games:** Use common household items to make homemade brain games for your Cavapoo. As an illustration, you could put sweets in a muffin tin and then cover each one with a tennis ball. To get to the treats, your Cavapoo must take out the balls, which exercises their problem-solving abilities.

You can keep your Cavapoo's mind sharp, prevent boredom, and give them an outlet for their instincts by incorporating regular mental stimulation into their daily routine.

In conclusion, regular exercise and mental stimulation are crucial components of preserving the general health, happiness, and wellbeing of your Cavapoo. You can make sure your Cavapoo stays active, engaged, and content by attending to their exercise needs, involving them in enjoyable activities and games, and offering mental stimulation through puzzle toys and training. Consider the individual needs and preferences of your Cavapoo when creating an exercise and mental stimulation plan because every dog is different. By doing this, you will deepen your relationship with your Cavapoo and benefit from a satisfying and balanced partnership.

CHAPTER 11:
AGING AND SENIOR CARE

Your Cavapoo's requirements will unavoidably change as they get older. You can make sure that your devoted companion leads a comfortable and rewarding life during their golden years by being aware of these changes and taking appropriate action. Identifying and addressing age-related changes, modifying exercise, diet, and grooming for senior Cavapoos, and offering comfort and support as they age are all topics covered in this chapter.

IDENTIFYING AND TAKING CARE OF AGE-RELATED CHANGES

Like all dogs, Cavapoos age and undergo a number of age-related changes. To ensure your dog's continued comfort and health, you can modify your care routine by recognizing these changes. The following are some typical age-related changes in Cavapoos:

1. **Lower Energy Levels:** Senior Cavapoos may have less energy than younger Cavapoos. Make sure to modify their exercise program to fit their evolving needs while continuing to provide plenty of opportunities for physical activity.

2. **Joint and Mobility Issues:** As they age, Cavapoos may experience joint and mobility problems like hip dysplasia or arthritis. In addition to changing your dog's environment and providing various supplements, medications, and care, regular veterinary care is crucial in managing these conditions.

3. **Cognitive Decline:** Older dogs may experience cognitive dysfunction syndrome (CDS), which is comparable to dementia in humans. Disorientation, adjustments to sleep patterns, and a reduction in family interaction are all symptoms. If your Cavapoo exhibits these changes, speak with your veterinarian

right away because there are treatments and medications that could help to enhance cognitive function.

4. **Vision and Hearing Loss:** As dogs age, they frequently experience vision and hearing loss that is age-related. Regular veterinary visits can help keep an eye on these modifications and offer advice on how to adapt your home to better accommodate a canine with sensory impairments.

5. **Weight Gain or Loss:** In older Cavapoos, changes in metabolism can cause weight gain or loss. Throughout your dog's senior years, regular weight monitoring and dietary and exercise modifications can help maintain a healthy weight.

6. **Dental Problems:** Older dogs are more prone to dental problems, such as tooth loss and gum disease. Keep up a consistent dental hygiene regimen and make frequent appointments with your veterinarian for dental examinations.

7. **Coat and Skin Changes:** The coat of your senior Cavapoo may get drier, thinner, and more prone to matting. Regular grooming can keep a coat healthy, and any skin problems that develop should receive special attention.

You can make sure your senior Cavapoo gets the proper care and attention they require to stay comfortable and healthy by identifying and addressing these age-related changes.

MODIFYING ACTIVITY, DIET, AND PERSONAL CARE FOR SENIOR CAVAPOOS

Your Cavapoo's exercise, dietary, and grooming regimens should be modified as they age to meet their evolving needs.

1. **Exercise:** Senior Cavapoos still need to be physically active on a regular basis, but a modified exercise program may be necessary due to potential physical limitations. Avoid overexerting your dog by focusing on low-impact activities like leisurely walks and gentle play. Keep an eye out for signs of fatigue or discomfort in your senior Cavapoo and modify their exercise routine as necessary.

2. **Diet:** Older dogs' diets, which typically contain fewer calories and are designed to support joint health and digestion, may be beneficial to senior Cavapoos. Ask your vet for advice on the best diet for your senior Cavapoo and take into account any special dietary requirements or restrictions, such as allergies or preexisting medical conditions.

3. **Grooming:** Your Cavapoo's grooming regimen may need to be adjusted as they age because their coat may change. Regular brushing can help prevent matting and distribute natural oils, but any skin problems that develop, like dryness or irritation, should receive special attention. Based on your dog's individual needs, adjust the frequency of bathing, being careful not to over-bathe them as this can cause their coat to lose its natural oils.

Your senior Cavapoo's exercise, eating, and grooming regimens can be modified to help them stay comfortable and healthy as they age.

PROVIDING SOLACE AND ASSISTANCE LATER IN LIFE

Your elderly Cavapoo will need more comfort and assistance as they age and enter their golden years. Here are some suggestions for making your elderly Cavapoo feel at home and supported:

1. **Orthopedic Bed:** An orthopedic bed can offer senior Cavapoos with joint and mobility problems the support and comfort they need. Look for beds with memory foam or other supportive materials to help your dog's joints by relieving pressure.

2. **Ramps and Stairs:** If your senior Cavapoo has trouble jumping onto furniture or climbing stairs, think about installing ramps or stairs to make these tasks simpler and lessen the stress on their joints.

3. **Body Temperature Control:** Older dogs may have trouble controlling their body temperatures, so make sure your Cavapoo has access to a cool, comfortable space in the summer and a warm, draft-free space in the winter.

4. **Regular Veterinary Exams:** Senior dogs may need more frequent veterinary examinations to monitor their general health and address any age-related problems. The frequency of your senior Cavapoo's checkups should be discussed with your veterinarian, so pay attention to their advice.

5. **Mental Stimulation:** To maintain cognitive health in your senior Cavapoo, mental stimulation is crucial. Continue to involve them in games and activities that are age-appropriate, and think about including puzzle toys and brain games to keep their minds active.

6. **Patience and Understanding:** As your Cavapoo ages, they might go through behavioral or temperamental changes as a result of pain in their bodies or cognitive decline. Give your senior dog the love and attention they require at this point in their life by being patient and understanding of their needs.

7. **End-of-Life Care:** It's important to openly discuss your senior Cavapoo's quality of life and end-of-life care with your veterinarian. Be prepared to give your dog the support and comfort they require in their final days and make informed decisions about your dog's care.

Finally, aging is a natural process that all dogs go through, so it's important to modify your care routine to accommodate your senior Cavapoo's changing needs. You can make sure your devoted companion stays healthy, content, and comfortable for the duration of their life by identifying and addressing age-related changes, adjusting exercise, diet, and grooming routines, and offering comfort and support during their senior years. Your Cavapoo will bring years of happiness and companionship to your family with your love and commitment.

MOURNING AND DEALING WITH LOSS

Losing a beloved pet is one of the most challenging experiences a pet owner can go through. It's essential to remember that grief is a natural response to such a loss, and everyone processes grief differently. This section aims to guide you through the mourning process and provide suggestions on how to cope with the loss of your cherished Cavapoo.

Acknowledge Your Grief: Grief can manifest in many forms, including sadness, anger, disbelief, guilt, and sometimes even relief, particularly if your pet was suffering. All these emotions are normal and important to acknowledge. Allow yourself to feel these emotions without judgment. It's an important part of the healing process.

Seek Support: Reach out to people who understand your loss. Friends, family, or pet-loss support groups can provide comfort during this difficult time. Consider seeking professional help if your grief feels overwhelming or unmanageable. Many counselors specialize in pet loss and can provide coping strategies.

Memorialize Your Pet: Creating a memorial can be a therapeutic way of processing your loss. This could be a photo album, a memory box with their favorite toys, or a special place in your garden. Some people also find comfort in hosting a small memorial service. Do whatever feels right for you.

Self-Care: Grief can be physically and mentally exhausting. Make sure to take care of yourself. Try to maintain a regular sleep schedule, eat healthily, and engage in physical activities. Mindfulness and relaxation techniques can also be beneficial during this time.

Consider a Pet Loss Support Hotline: Some organizations offer pet loss hotlines staffed by trained professionals who can provide immediate support and guidance.

Be Patient With Yourself: Healing takes time, and it's different for everyone. Allow yourself the time you need to grieve and heal. It's okay to have good days and bad days.

Helping Children Cope: If you have children, it's important to help them understand and cope with the loss. Be honest with them about what has happened in a way that is appropriate for their age. Encourage them to express their feelings and remember their pet in their own way.

Other Pets Grieving: Pets can grieve too. If you have other pets, they may show signs of distress or confusion. Maintain their routines as much as possible and give them extra attention and love.

When to Get Another Pet: There's no right or wrong time to get another pet — it's a personal decision that should be made when you feel ready. Some people find comfort in getting another pet soon after their loss, while others need more time to grieve. It's crucial to remember that getting another pet is not about replacing your lost one but about opening your home and heart to another animal in need.

Remember, it's okay to grieve, and it's okay to cry. Your Cavapoo was a beloved member of your family, and it's natural to feel a deep sense of loss. Be gentle with yourself and seek support as you navigate this difficult time.

CHAPTER 12:
THE CAVAPOO COMMUNITY
& SUPPORT

Following your education on how to raise, discipline, and care for your Cavapoo, you may want to get in touch with other Cavapoo owners and enthusiasts. This chapter will go over the advantages of becoming a part of the Cavapoo community, taking part in breed-specific activities and clubs, and researching online resources and support networks.

GETTING IN TOUCH WITH OTHER CAVAPOO OWNERS

The chance to interact with people who share your love and passion for the breed is one of the most fulfilling aspects of owning a Cavapoo. Engaging with other Cavapoo owners allows you to exchange experiences, counsel, and support, which will make you a more knowledgeable and assured dog owner.

To get in touch with other Cavapoo owners, try these methods:

1. **Participate in neighborhood dog events and meetups:** Look for dog-related events in your area, such as pet expos, dog shows, and breed-specific meetups, on the community calendar. These events give you the chance to socialize with other Cavapoo owners and enthusiasts, and you might even learn about new things to do with your pet.

2. **Establish a connection on social media:** There are many Cavapoo-specific groups and pages on websites like Facebook, Instagram, and Twitter. You can interact with other Cavapoo owners in these communities, exchange photos and stories, and ask questions or look for guidance on a variety of matters relating to Cavapoo ownership by joining these communities.

3. **Enroll in obedience and training classes:** Meeting other dog owners and their pets can be a lot of fun and educational when you take obedience and training classes. There may even be other Cavapoo owners in your class, giving you the chance

to form relationships and friendships with people who share your interests.

4. **Volunteer at neighborhood animal shelters and rescue groups:** Many animal shelters and rescue groups offer volunteer opportunities to help with pet care and adoption occasions. By volunteering, you can meet other dog lovers and possibly other Cavapoo owners in addition to helping animals in need.

PARTICIPATING IN CLUBS AND EVENTS SPECIFIC TO YOUR BREED

Although major kennel clubs have not yet recognized Cavapoos as an official breed, there are still many breed-specific gatherings and clubs you can join to celebrate and show off your Cavapoo. These gatherings are great places to get to know other Cavapoo fans and learn more about the breed.

1. **Cavapoo Meetups and Playdates:** Arrange or go to neighborhood Cavapoo get-togethers, playdates, or picnics. These events give your Cavapoo the chance to interact with other Cavapoos of the same breed while you connect with other Cavapoo owners and swap stories, advice, and tips.

2. **Competitions in Agility and Obedience:** Cavapoos excel in agility and obedience events thanks to their intelligence and athleticism. These occasions give you the chance to not only show off your Cavapoo's talents but also to interact with other dog owners and bond with your pet.

3. **Therapy Dog Work:** Cavapoos make wonderful candidates for therapy dog work due to their amiable and affectionate nature. Enlisting your Cavapoo in a therapy dog program

can be rewarding for both you and your dog and give you the opportunity to cheer up people in need.

4. **Cavapoo-Specific Clubs:** Although there may not yet be official breed clubs for the Cavapoo, you can still look for or start local discussion groups or clubs to meet other Cavapoo enthusiasts. These organizations can offer you opportunities to connect with like-minded people while also offering you support and camaraderie.

ONLINE TOOLS AND SUPPORT NETWORKS

The internet has a wealth of information on Cavapoos, from blogs and websites with educational content to forums and support groups. These online communities offer a platform for interaction with other Cavapoo enthusiasts from around the world as well as valuable information and advice.

Following are a few online resources and forums for Cavapoo owners:

1. **Cavapoo-specific Facebook groups:** These online communities provide a welcoming and lively forum for Cavapoo owners to share experiences, pose queries, and look for guidance. Find groups on Facebook by searching "Cavapoo" to find ones that suit your requirements and interests.

2. **Online forums:** Websites like Reddit and forums devoted to pets frequently have threads and discussion boards devoted to Cavapoos, giving you a place to pose queries, talk about problems, and post pictures and memories of your cherished pet.

3. **Blogs and Websites:** A lot of blogs and websites offer guidance and information on Cavapoo ownership, training,

and care. The Happy Puppy Site, Your Dog Advisor, and Perfect Dog Breeds are a few examples. These websites are great places to learn more about Cavapoos and deepen your understanding of the breed.

4. **YouTube Channels:** If you learn best visually, many YouTube channels have informative videos on how to take care of, groom, train, and more for Cavapoos. You can access a wide variety of content that can advance your comprehension of Cavapoo ownership and care by subscribing to these channels.

FREQUENTLY ASKED QUESTIONS AND TROUBLESHOOTING:

1. **"Why does my Cavapoo bark so much?"** Cavapoos are generally known to be relatively quiet dogs, but if you're experiencing excessive barking, there could be a few reasons. It could be due to boredom, attention-seeking, or even fear. To mitigate this, ensure your Cavapoo is getting enough mental and physical exercise, establish a routine, and consider training methods to manage barking. Remember, consistency is key.

2. **"Why is my Cavapoo so picky with food?"** Cavapoos can sometimes be picky eaters. It's important to ensure they are not being fed too many treats, which can make them less interested in their regular food. Also, sudden changes in their diet can make them finicky. Try transitioning slowly if you are changing their food, and if you're still having trouble, consult with your vet for advice. Likewise, it can be helpful to stick to a very clear feeding routine and schedule, and even remove the food after several minutes if it's left uneaten. That can send a clearer signal to your Cavapoo to eat at the times set by you.

3. **"Why does my Cavapoo have tear stains?"** Tear staining is quite common in Cavapoos due to their big, expressive eyes. It could be due to a variety of reasons such as allergies, blocked tear ducts, or even diet. Regular face washing and grooming can help reduce tear stains. However, if you notice excessive tearing or other eye problems, it's best to consult with a vet.

4. **"Why does my Cavapoo shed so much?"** Despite having Poodle heritage, Cavapoos can still shed. The amount usually depends on whether they inherited more of their coat characteristics from the Cavalier King Charles Spaniel or the Poodle. Regular brushing can help manage shedding. If you notice excessive or sudden hair loss, it's best to consult a vet as it could indicate a health issue.

5. **"Is it normal for my Cavapoo to be so hyperactive?"** Cavapoos are known to be lively and energetic, especially as puppies. Regular exercise, both physical and mental, can help manage their energy levels. If you're struggling with hyperactivity, it could be a sign that your Cavapoo isn't getting enough stimulation or exercise. Structured playtimes, walks, and training sessions can help tire them out and reduce hyperactive behavior.

6. **"My Cavapoo seems to get anxious when I leave. What can I do?"** Cavapoos are a breed known for their strong attachment to their owners, which can sometimes result in separation anxiety. Establishing a predictable routine can help, as can slowly increasing the amount of time they spend alone. Training your Cavapoo to associate your departures with positive experiences, such as receiving a treat or a favorite

toy, can also be beneficial. In severe cases, a professional dog behaviorist or a veterinarian could provide further guidance.

7. **"Why does my Cavapoo keep digging holes in the yard?"** While not a breed-specific behavior, some Cavapoos might engage in digging due to their energetic nature. They may be bored, seeking entertainment, or even trying to create a cool spot to lie in during hot weather. Providing alternative activities, like toys or playtime, can help redirect this behavior. If it becomes a persistent issue, consult with a professional trainer to understand the root cause and develop a solution.

8. **"My Cavapoo seems to scratch a lot, but I don't see any fleas. What could be the issue?"** If your Cavapoo is scratching excessively but there are no signs of fleas, it could be due to a variety of reasons such as dry skin, allergies, or even an underlying health issue. Regular grooming and a balanced diet can help maintain healthy skin and coat. However, if the scratching continues or if your Cavapoo seems uncomfortable, it's best to consult a vet for a thorough examination.

You can deepen your appreciation for your Cavapoo, learn more about the breed, and meet like-minded people by taking part in the Cavapoo community, both in person and online. Your life will be enriched by the connections you make with other Cavapoo lovers and your pet, and you'll have enduring memories and experiences to look back on.

THANK YOU

Cavapoos make wonderful companions and bring their families laughter, love, and joy. You can create a happy and nurturing environment for your Cavapoo by being aware of their special traits, background, and needs. In this book, we've covered a variety of topics related to caring for a Cavapoo, such as picking the best puppy or rescue, setting up a secure environment at home, developing a close relationship with your pet, and attending to your dog's nutritional, veterinary, training, and exercise requirements.

Remember that patience, consistency, and love are the keys to raising a well-adjusted and content dog as you navigate the ups and downs of owning a Cavapoo. Accept the responsibilities and rewards that come with raising a Cavapoo and treasure the unique relationship you will develop with your pet.

You can continue to increase your understanding of and admiration for this unusual and endearing breed by getting involved in the Cavapoo community and interacting with other Cavapoo owners and enthusiasts. You will develop into an even more self-assured, encouraging, and prosperous Cavapoo owner as you make new acquaintances and friendships.

We trust "The Cavapoo Way: A Guide to Successful Dog Ownership" has given you the knowledge, direction, and motivation you require to start a fulfilling and enjoyable journey with your Cavapoo. May the road ahead be paved with wagging tails, wet noses, and unending love.

Printed in Great Britain
by Amazon

28935152R00056